GREEN BAY PACKERS

NICK REBMAN

WWW.APEXEDITIONS.COM

Apex is distributed by North Star Editions:
sales@northstareditions.com | 888-417-0195

Produced for Apex by Red Line Editorial.

Photographs ©: Jeffrey Phelps/AP Images, cover, 1; Jonathan Daniel/Getty Images Sport/Getty Images, 4–5, 6–7, 42–43; Shutterstock Images, 8–9, 48–49; Sports Studio Photos/Getty Images Sport/Getty Images, 10–11; Bettmann/Getty Images, 12–13, 16–17; Focus On Sport/Getty Images Sport/Getty Images, 14–15, 26–27, 30–31; Tony Tomsic/AP Images, 19, 58–59; Robert Walsh/AP Images, 20–21; James Flores/Getty Images Sport/Getty Images, 22–23, 24–25; Ronald C. Modra/Getty Images Sport/Getty Images, 28–29; Tony Medina/Icon Sportswire, 32–33; Christian Petersen/Getty Images Sport/Getty Images, 34–35; Charles Krupa/AP Images, 37; Joe Robbins/AP Images, 38–39, 57; Stacy Revere/Getty Images Sport/Getty Images, 40–41; Patrick McDermott/Getty Images Sport/Getty Images, 44–45; Robin Alam/Icon Sportswire, 47; Morry Gash/AP Images, 50–51; Larry Radloff/Icon Sportswire, 52–53; Allen Fredrickson/Icon Sportswire, 54–55

Library of Congress Control Number: 2023922695

ISBN
979-8-89250-083-8 (hardcover)
979-8-89250-100-2 (paperback)
979-8-89250-133-0 (ebook pdf)
979-8-89250-117-0 (hosted ebook)

Printed in the United States of America
Mankato, MN
082024

NOTE TO PARENTS AND EDUCATORS

Apex books are designed to build literacy skills in striving readers. Exciting, high-interest content attracts and holds readers' attention. The text is carefully leveled to allow students to achieve success quickly.

TABLE OF CONTENTS

CHAPTER 1

GO PACK GO!

Thousands of football fans rise to their feet. They cheer for the Green Bay Packers. The city of Green Bay, Wisconsin, is known as Titletown. That's because the Packers have won so many NFL championships. No team has won more.

During Packers home games, the chant "Go Pack Go!" echoes through the stadium.

Many fans refer to the Packers' playing field as the "frozen tundra."

Snow begins to fall. It drifts down onto the turf. Soon, the Packers score a touchdown. The player who scored jumps into the crowd. The fans dance and sing.

SMALL CITY, BIG STADIUM

Green Bay is the smallest NFL city by far. The population is only 107,000. However, the Packers play in one of the league's biggest stadiums. It holds more than 81,000 fans.

CHAPTER 2

EARLY HISTORY

The Packers played their first season in 1919. Curly Lambeau helped start the team. He worked for a local meat-packing company. The company gave him money for the team's uniforms. That's why the team became known as the Packers.

Today, a statue of Curly Lambeau stands outside the Packers' stadium. The stadium is called Lambeau Field in his honor.

The Packers did not play in the NFL at first. That's because the league didn't exist yet. The Packers played other independent teams. Most games took place in Wisconsin.

The Packers pose for a team photo in 1921. The team was supported by the Acme Packing Company.

JOINING THE NFL

The NFL formed in 1920. But the Packers didn't join the league until 1921. That year, the NFL had 21 teams. Green Bay finished in seventh place.

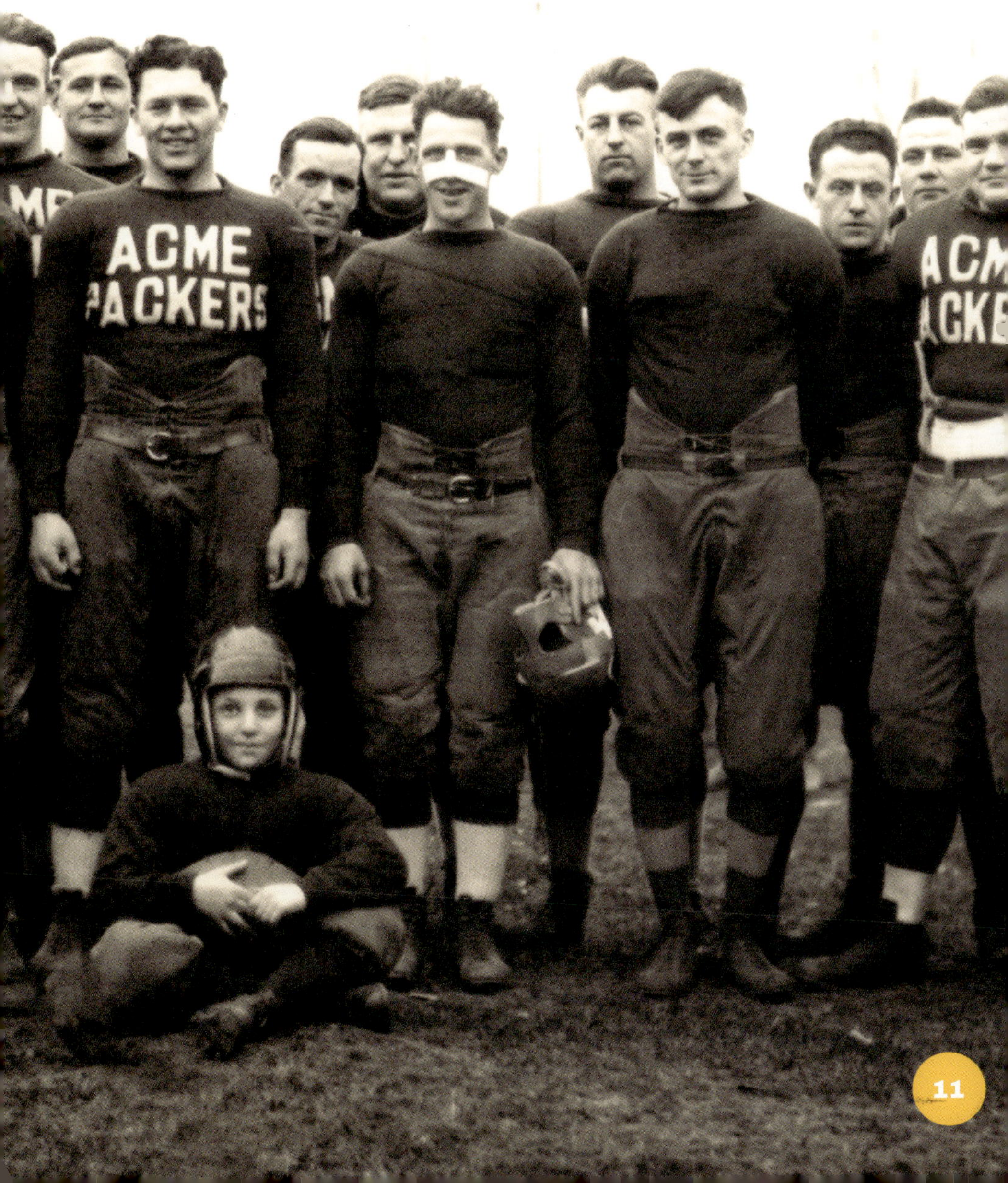

The Packers take on the New York Giants in the 1939 NFL Championship Game.

Green Bay was an average team for most of the 1920s. But things soon changed. The Packers won five NFL titles between 1929 and 1939. They added another in 1944. Curly Lambeau had built a dynasty.

A LONG RIVALRY

Green Bay has a heated rivalry with the Chicago Bears. Like the Packers, the Bears are one of the oldest teams in the NFL. The two teams have played each other more than 200 times.

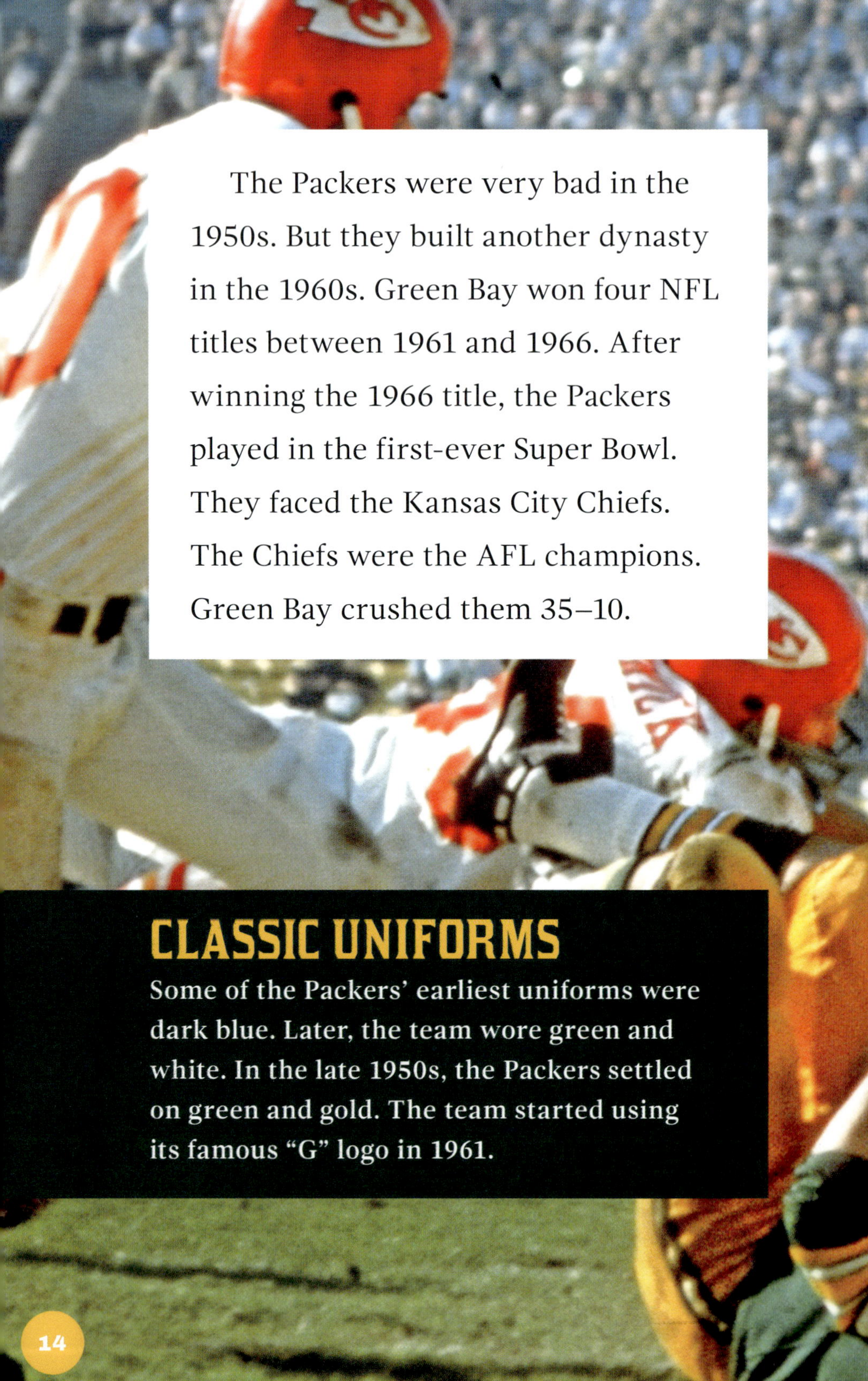

The Packers were very bad in the 1950s. But they built another dynasty in the 1960s. Green Bay won four NFL titles between 1961 and 1966. After winning the 1966 title, the Packers played in the first-ever Super Bowl. They faced the Kansas City Chiefs. The Chiefs were the AFL champions. Green Bay crushed them 35–10.

CLASSIC UNIFORMS

Some of the Packers' earliest uniforms were dark blue. Later, the team wore green and white. In the late 1950s, the Packers settled on green and gold. The team started using its famous "G" logo in 1961.

The AFL was a separate league from 1960 to 1969. It joined the NFL in 1970.

Bart Starr (15) scores the winning touchdown against the Dallas Cowboys in the 1967 NFL Championship Game.

In 1967, the Packers reached the NFL title game again. They faced the Dallas Cowboys. The temperature was far below zero. The game became known as the Ice Bowl. With only 13 seconds to go, Green Bay scored the winning touchdown. It was the team's fifth NFL title in seven years. Two weeks later, the Packers won their second Super Bowl. They beat the Oakland Raiders 33–14.

COACH SPOTLIGHT

VINCE LOMBARDI

Vince Lombardi became Green Bay's head coach in 1959. At that time, the Packers were terrible. But Lombardi turned the team around. He never had a losing season. He helped the Packers become the best team of the 1960s.

Lombardi demanded greatness from his players. He also demanded fairness. Lombardi signed more Black players than most other coaches of the era. He also got rid of white players who didn't accept their Black teammates.

"ONCE YOU LEARN TO QUIT, IT BECOMES A HABIT."
–VINCE LOMBARDI

CHAPTER 3

LEGENDS

The Packers have had many great players. In the 1930s and 1940s, Don Hutson was the NFL's best receiver. He came up with many routes. Receivers still use them today.

Tony Canadeo led on the ground. In 1949, he became the fourth NFL player to top 1,000 rushing yards.

Don Hutson set several NFL receiving records during his 11-year career.

Bart Starr (15) threw 152 touchdown passes during his 16 years with the Packers.

Quarterback Bart Starr led Green Bay's passing attack in the 1960s. Starr won the Most Valuable Player (MVP) Award in the first two Super Bowls. And in 1967, he scored the winning touchdown in the Ice Bowl. It was a quarterback sneak.

STAR RECEIVER

Bart Starr threw two touchdown passes in the first Super Bowl. Max McGee caught both of them. The wide receiver played 12 seasons with the Packers. Later, McGee spent many years as the team's radio announcer.

In the 1960s, opponents feared Green Bay's running game. Jim Taylor was known for slamming into defenders. He racked up 1,000 yards five years in a row.

Paul Hornung was another powerful runner. He led the league in scoring for three straight seasons.

THE PACKERS SWEEP

In the 1960s, Green Bay had excellent blockers. They cleared paths so Jim Taylor and Paul Hornung could run. One play became known as the Packers Sweep. Defenders knew it was coming. But they couldn't stop it.

Jim Taylor (31) runs the Packers Sweep during the first Super Bowl.

Willie Davis led Green Bay's defense in the 1960s. Davis was known for taking down quarterbacks. He was great at recovering fumbles, too.

Ray Nitschke was one of the NFL's hardest tacklers. He also made many interceptions.

INTERCEPTION EXPERT

Herb Adderley was another legend of the Packers' 1960s defense. He grabbed dozens of interceptions. He ran many of them back for touchdowns, too.

Willie Davis (87) had three sacks in the Super Bowl against the Oakland Raiders.

CHAPTER 4

RECENT HISTORY

The 1970s and 1980s were tough times for the Packers. The team had many losing seasons. The glory days of the 1960s were a distant memory. But fans still filled the stadium every Sunday.

Quarterback Lynn Dickey (12) led Green Bay's offense from the late 1970s to the mid-1980s.

Desmond Howard (81) returns a kickoff during the Super Bowl.

Quarterback Brett Favre joined the team in 1992. Green Bay soon returned to greatness. In 1996, the Packers had the NFL's best offense. They also had the league's best defense. That season, Green Bay won its third Super Bowl.

SPECIAL TEAMS

Green Bay also had one of the league's best special teams units in 1996. That came in handy during the Super Bowl. Desmond Howard returned a kickoff 99 yards. He was named the MVP of the game. The Packers beat the New England Patriots 35–21.

Wide receiver Greg Jennings (85) scored two touchdowns in the Super Bowl.

In 2008, Aaron Rodgers became Green Bay's new starting quarterback. He helped maintain the team's winning ways. In the 2010 season, the Packers won their fourth Super Bowl. They beat the Pittsburgh Steelers 31–25.

WINNING THE HARD WAY

The 2010 Packers were the lowest seed in the playoffs. So, they had to play all three of their games on the road. The Packers won them all. That included a victory over the Chicago Bears.

Aaron Rodgers (12) attempts a pass in the 2014 conference championship game.

The Packers were loaded with talent all through the 2010s. They made the playoffs in eight of ten seasons. But Green Bay often struggled in the playoffs. One example came in the 2014 season. The Packers reached the conference championship game. They faced the Seattle Seahawks. Green Bay led 19–7 in the fourth quarter. But the Seahawks came back. The Packers lost in overtime.

PLAYER SPOTLIGHT

REGGIE WHITE

Reggie White started his NFL career with the Philadelphia Eagles. He soon became one of the best defensive ends in the league. In 1993, White was a free agent. That meant he could join any team. Few people expected him to choose Green Bay. The Packers had missed the playoffs for 10 straight seasons. However, White believed the team was on the rise.

White spent six years with the Packers. In the 1996 season, he helped them win the Super Bowl. White recorded three sacks in the game.

REGGIE WHITE TALLIED 68.5 SACKS DURING HIS SIX SEASONS WITH GREEN BAY.

Riddell
92

CHAPTER 5

MODERN STARS

Few players were more exciting than Brett Favre. The star quarterback led many thrilling comebacks. He was also as tough as they come. Favre started 253 straight games with the Packers. He often passed to wide receiver Antonio Freeman. They connected for 57 touchdowns.

Brett Favre played for the Packers from 1992 to 2007.

Davante Adams (17) hauls in a pass from Aaron Rodgers.

Favre left Green Bay after the 2007 season. But the Packers already had another star in the making. Aaron Rodgers became one of the best quarterbacks in NFL history. He tossed 475 touchdown passes as a Packer. That was a team record.

RECORD SEASON

Aaron Rodgers often threw to Davante Adams. The star receiver spent eight years with the Packers. In 2020, Adams tied a team record. He caught 18 touchdown passes that season.

Charles Woodson (21) recorded 38 interceptions for the Packers.

On defense, Charles Woodson was one of the team's best players. He was also a great leader. In the 2010 season, Woodson helped Green Bay reach the Super Bowl. At halftime, he gave a powerful speech to his team. The Packers went on to win the game.

SACK MASTER

In the 2010s, Clay Matthews was Green Bay's star linebacker. Matthews had a knack for getting to the quarterback. He recorded 83.5 sacks with the Packers. Matthews also made the Pro Bowl six times.

PACKERS
NFL
10
NFL

A new era began in 2023. Jordan Love became the team's starting quarterback. He led Green Bay to the playoffs that season. Packers fans hoped it wouldn't be long before the team was back in the Super Bowl.

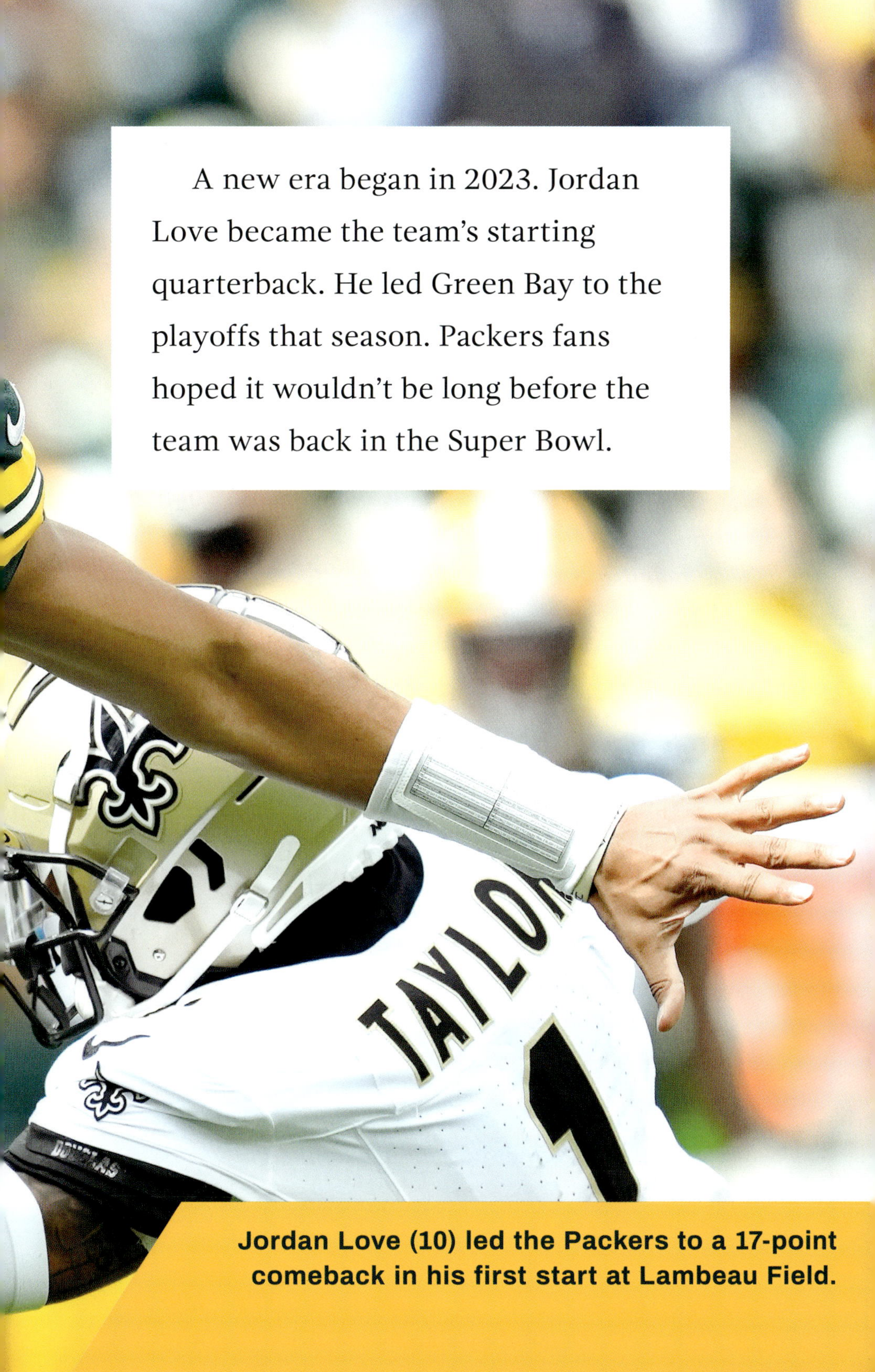

Jordan Love (10) led the Packers to a 17-point comeback in his first start at Lambeau Field.

PLAYER SPOTLIGHT

AARON RODGERS

Aaron Rodgers joined the Packers in 2005. At first, he served as a backup. But in 2008, he got his chance to start. Two years later, he helped Green Bay win the Super Bowl.

Rodgers had a very strong arm. He also had amazing accuracy. So, he didn't throw many interceptions. Rodgers spent 15 years as Green Bay's starting quarterback. In that time, he won four MVP Awards. The Packers made the playoffs 11 times.

AARON RODGERS THREW FOR MORE THAN 59,000 YARDS DURING HIS 18 YEARS WITH THE PACKERS.

12
adidas

CHAPTER 6

TEAM TRIVIA

The Packers play at Lambeau Field. It is one of the most famous stadiums in sports. The Packers Hall of Fame is attached to the stadium. Here, fans can learn about the team's history.

Lambeau Field doesn't have a roof. So, games can be very cold during the winter.

The Packers' bike tradition gives kids a chance to talk to players.

The Packers have sold out every game at Lambeau Field since 1959. The waiting list for season tickets is decades long. So, Packers fans often travel to away games. For many people, that's the only way to see the team play.

TRAINING CAMP TRADITION

During training camp, kids let players ride their bikes. The players ride between the practice field and the locker room. This tradition dates back to the 1950s.

Packers fans are known for their passion and loyalty. The fans are called Cheeseheads. That's because Wisconsin is famous for its cheese. Some fans even wear hats that look like cheese.

PREGAME PARTIES

Every Packers home game is an all-day event. Many fans arrive hours before the game starts. They set up grills in the parking lot. The smell of bratwurst fills the air.

Packers fans' loud cheering makes Lambeau Field a tough place for opponents to play.

Dozens of players have done the Lambeau Leap over the years.

Packers players often jump into the crowd after scoring. That's called the Lambeau Leap. The stadium also plays "Bang the Drum All Day" after touchdowns. And after the third quarter, fans sing and dance to a polka song.

PUBLICLY OWNED

The Packers are the only publicly owned team in the NFL. That means there isn't a single owner. Instead, fans can buy stock in the team. More than half a million people own it.

TEAM RECORDS

All-Time Passing Yards: 61,655
Brett Favre (1992–2007)

All-Time Touchdown Passes: 475
Aaron Rodgers (2005–22)

All-Time Rushing Yards: 8,322
Ahman Green (2000–06, 2009)

All-Time Receiving Yards: 10,137
Donald Driver (1999–2012)

All-Time Interceptions: 52
Bobby Dillon (1952–59)

All-Time Sacks: 99.5*
Willie Davis (1960–69)

All-Time Scoring: 1,918
Mason Crosby (2007–22)

All-Time Coaching Wins: 209
Curly Lambeau (1921–49)

NFL Titles: 9
(1929, 1930, 1931, 1936, 1939, 1944, 1961, 1962, 1965)

Super Bowl Titles: 4
(1966, 1967, 1996, 2010)

** Sacks were not an official statistic until 1982. However, researchers have studied old games to determine sacks dating back to 1960.*

All statistics are accurate through 2023.

Riddell
4
LAMBEAU FIELD
NATIONAL FOOTBALL LEAGUE
Wilson

TIMELINE

1919
Curly Lambeau helps start the Packers.

1921
The Packers join the NFL.

1931
The Packers become the first team to win three straight NFL titles.

1957
Lambeau Field opens. In their first game at the new stadium, the Packers defeat the Chicago Bears.

1967
The Packers win their fifth NFL title in seven years. They also win their second Super Bowl in a row.

1993
After scoring a touchdown, LeRoy Butler does the first-ever Lambeau Leap.

1996
The Packers win their third Super Bowl. It's the team's first championship in nearly three decades.

1997
Brett Favre wins the MVP Award for the third straight season.

2010
Green Bay wins its fourth Super Bowl title.

2021
Aaron Rodgers wins the MVP Award for the fourth time in his career.

COMPREHENSION QUESTIONS

Write your answers on a separate piece of paper.

1. Write a paragraph that explains the main ideas of Chapter 2.

2. Who do you think was the greatest player in Green Bay Packers history? Why?

3. Who helped start the Packers in 1919?

A. Curly Lambeau
B. Vince Lombardi
C. Aaron Rodgers

4. Why is accuracy important for quarterbacks?

A. because accurate passes are often intercepted
B. because accurate passes go as far as possible
C. because accurate passes will reach the right receiver

5. What does **maintain** mean in this book?

He helped ***maintain*** *the team's winning ways. In the 2010 season, the Packers won their fourth Super Bowl.*

A. to bring something to an end
B. to keep something going
C. to make something harder

6. What does **knack** mean in this book?

Matthews had a ***knack*** *for getting to the quarterback. He recorded 83.5 sacks with the Packers.*

A. skill or talent
B. no talent
C. amount of time

Answer key on page 64.

GLOSSARY

conference
A group of teams that make up part of a sports league.

dynasty
A team that has a long period of success. The team usually wins several championships.

independent
Not part of a league.

league
A group of teams that play one another and compete for a championship.

rivalry
An ongoing competition that brings out strong emotion from fans and players.

routes
Paths that receivers take so they can get open and catch the ball.

sacks
Plays that happen when a defender tackles the quarterback before he can throw the ball.

seed
A team's ranking heading into a tournament.

special teams
The players on the field during kicks and punts.

stock
Part ownership of a company.

tradition
A way of doing something that is passed down over many years.

TO LEARN MORE

BOOKS

Abdo, Kenny. *Green Bay Packers*. Minneapolis: Abdo Publishing, 2022.

Anderson, Josh. *Inside the Green Bay Packers*. Minneapolis: Lerner Publications, 2024.

Chandler, Matt. *Football's Greatest Hail Mary Passes and Other Crunch-Time Heroics*. North Mankato, MN: Capstone Press, 2021.

ONLINE RESOURCES

Visit **www.apexeditions.com** to find links and resources related to this title.

ABOUT THE AUTHOR

Nick Rebman is the author of dozens of educational children's books. He grew up in Green Bay, less than a mile from Lambeau Field. Today he lives in Minnesota, where everyone cheers for the wrong team.

INDEX

ANSWER KEY:

1. Answers will vary; 2. Answers will vary; 3. A; 4. C; 5. B; 6. A